BECOMING MUSLIM

❊

NUH HA MIM KELLER

With an appendix of al-Ghazali's
THE MUSLIM BELIEF IN GOD

WAKEEL BOOKS
AMMAN

WAKEEL BOOKS

P.O. BOX 962660, AMMAN 11196, JORDAN

www.wakeelbooks.com

ISBN 9957-23-003-4

Cover photo by Nabeel Turner / © Stone

Printed in Jordan

PREFACE

Someone asked me to write the story of how I entered Islam, what it was that I liked about the religion, and what motivated me to become a Muslim. Now, stories have a beginning, middle, and end, while life is not often so simple. One's course is seldom determined, particularly in events of the mind and heart, by causes and effects few enough to fit into a tale. But deficient as such an account must be, it may yet prove of interest to a now largely despiritualized world that sees only a "play of forces"; if only to acknowledge the hand of Allah, and if He will, to reach those who aspire to more than they find around them.

بِسْمِ اللَّهِ الرَّحْمَٰنِ الرَّحِيمِ

In the Name of Allah, Most Merciful and Compassionate

B ORN in 1954 in the farm country of the northwestern
United States, I was raised in a religious family as a
Roman Catholic. The Church provided a spiritual world
that was unquestionable in my childhood, if anything
more real than the physical world around me, but as I
grew older, and especially after I entered a Catholic university and read more, my relation to the religion became
increasingly called into question, in belief and practice.

One reason was the frequent changes in Catholic liturgy
and ritual that occurred in the wake of the Second Vatican
Council of 1963, suggesting to laymen that the Church
had no firm standards. To one another, the clergy spoke
about "flexibility" and "liturgical relevance," but to
ordinary Catholics they seemed to be groping in the
dark. God does not change, nor the needs of the human
soul, and there was no new revelation from heaven. Yet
we rang in the changes, week after week, year after year;
adding, subtracting, changing the language from Latin to
English, finally bringing in guitars and folk music. Priests
explained and explained as laymen shook their heads.
The search for relevance left large numbers convinced
that there had not been much in the first place.

5

A second reason was a number of doctrinal difficulties, such as the doctrine of the Trinity, which no one in the history of the world, neither priest nor layman, had been able to explain in a convincing way, and which resolved itself, to the common mind at least, in a sort of godhead-by-committee, shared between God the Father, who ruled the world from heaven; His son Jesus Christ, who saved humanity on earth; and the Holy Ghost, who was pictured as a white dove and appeared to have a relatively lesser role. I remember wanting to make special friends with just one of them so he could handle my business with the others, and to this end, would sometimes pray earnestly to this one and sometimes to that; but the other two were always stubbornly there. I finally decided that God the Father must be in charge of the other two, and this put the most formidable obstacle in the way of my Catholicism, the divinity of Christ. Moreover, reflection made it plain that the nature of man contradicted the nature of God in every particular, the limitary and finite on the one hand, the absolute and infinite on the other. That Jesus was God was something I cannot remember having ever really believed, in childhood or later.

Another point of incredulity was the trading of the Church in stocks and bonds in the hereafter it called indulgences—"Do such and such and so-and-so many years will be remitted from your sentence in purgatory"— that had seemed so false to Martin Luther at the outset of the Reformation.

I also remember a desire for a sacred scripture, something on the order of a book that could furnish guidance.

A Bible was given to me one Christmas, a handsome edition, but on attempting to read it, I found it so rambling and devoid of a coherent thread that it was difficult to think of a way to base one's life upon it. Only later did I learn how Christians solve the difficulty in practice, Protestants by creating sectarian theologies, each emphasizing the texts of their sect and downplaying the rest; Catholics by downplaying it all, except the snippets mentioned in their liturgy. Something seemed lacking in a sacred book that could not be read as an integral whole.

Moreover, when I went to the university, I found that the authenticity of the book, especially the New Testament, had come into considerable doubt as a result of modern hermeneutical studies by Christians themselves. In a course on contemporary theology, I read the Norman Perrin translation of *The Problem of the Historical Jesus* by Joachim Jeremias, one of the principal New Testament scholars of this century. A textual critic who was a master of the original languages and had spent long years with the texts, he had finally agreed with the German theologian Rudolph Bultmann that "without a doubt it is true to say that the dream of ever writing a biography of Jesus is over," meaning that the life of Christ as he actually lived it cannot be reconstructed from the New Testament with any degree of confidence. If this were accepted from a friend of Christianity and one of its foremost textual experts, I reasoned, what was left for its enemies to say? And what then remained of the Bible except to acknowledge that it was a record of truths mixed with fictions, conjectures projected onto Christ by later followers,

7

themselves at odds with each other as to who the master had been and what he had taught. And if theologians like Jeremias could reassure themselves that somewhere under the layers of later accretions to the New Testament there was something called "the historical Jesus and his message," how could the ordinary person hope to find it, or know it, should it be found?

I studied philosophy at the university and it taught me to ask two things of whoever claimed to have the truth: What do you mean, and how do you know? When I asked these questions of my own religious tradition, I found no answers, and realized that Christianity had slipped from my hands. I then embarked on a search that is perhaps not unfamiliar to many young people in the West, a quest for meaning in a meaningless world.

I began where I had lost my previous belief, with the philosophers, yet wanting to believe, seeking not philosophy, but rather *a* philosophy.

I read the essays of the great pessimist Arthur Schopenhauer, which taught about the phenomenon of the ages of life, and that money, fame, physical strength, and intelligence all passed from one with the passage of years, but only moral excellence remained. I took this lesson to heart and remembered it in after years. His essays also drew attention to the fact that a person is wont to repudiate in later years what he fervently espouses in the heat of youth. With a prescient wish to find the Divine, I decided to imbue myself with the most cogent arguments of atheism that I could find, that perhaps I might find a way out of them later. So I read the Walter Kaufmann translations of the works of the immoralist Friedrich Nietzsche. The many-faceted genius dissected the moral judgments and beliefs of mankind with brilliant philological and psychological arguments that ended in accusing human language itself, and the language of nineteenth-century science in particular, of being so inherently determined and mediated by concepts inherited from the language of morality that in their present form they could never hope to uncover reality. Aside from their immunological value against total skepticism, Nietzsche's works explained why the West was post-Christian, and accurately predicted the unprecedented savagery of the twentieth century, debunking the myth that science could function as a moral replacement for the now dead religion.

At a personal level, his tirades against Christianity, particularly in *The Genealogy of Morals,* gave me the benefit of distilling the beliefs of the monotheistic tradition into a small number of analyzable forms. He separated unessential concepts (such as the bizarre spectacle of an omnipotent deity's suicide on the cross) from essential ones, which I now, though without believing in them, apprehended to be but three alone: that God existed; that He created man in the world and defined the conduct expected of him in it; and that He would judge man accordingly in the hereafter and send him to eternal reward or punishment.

It was during this time that I read an early translation of the Koran which I grudgingly admired, between agnostic reservations, for the purity with which it presented these fundamental concepts. "Even if false," I thought, "there could not be a more essential expression of religion." As a literary work, the translation, perhaps it was Sale's, was uninspired and openly hostile to its subject matter, whereas I knew the Arabic original was widely acknowledged for its beauty and eloquence among the religious books of mankind. I felt a desire to learn Arabic to read the original.

On a vacation home from school, I was walking upon a dirt road between some fields of wheat, and it happened that the sun went down. By some inspiration, I realized that it was a time of worship, a time to bow and pray to the one God. But it was not something one could rely on oneself to provide the details of, but rather a passing fancy, or perhaps the beginning of an awareness that atheism was an inauthentic way of being.

I carried something of this disquiet with me when I transferred to the University of Chicago, where I studied the epistemology of ethical theory—how moral judgments were reached—reading and searching among the books of the philosophers for something to shed light on the question of meaninglessness, which was both a personal concern and one of the central philosophical problems of our age.

According to some, scientific observation could only yield description statements of the form "X is Y," for example, "The object is red," "Its weight is two kilos," "Its height is ten centimeters," and so on, in each of which the functional was a scientifically verifiable *is*, whereas in moral judgments the functional element was an *ought*, a description statement which no amount of scientific observation could measure or verify. It appeared that *ought* was logically meaningless, and with it all morality whatsoever, a position that reminded me of those described by Lucian in his advice that whoever sees a moral philosopher coming down the road should flee from him as from a mad dog. For such a person, expediency ruled, and nothing checked his behavior but convention.

As Chicago was a more expensive school, and I had to raise tuition money, I found summer work on the West Coast with a seining boat fishing in Alaska. The sea proved a school in its own right, one I was to return to for a space of eight seasons, for the money. I met many people on boats, and saw something of the power and greatness of the wind, water, storms, and rain; and the smallness of man. These things lay before us like an immense book, but my fellow fishermen and I could only discern the letters of it that were within our context: to catch as many fish as possible within the specified time to sell to the tenders. Few knew how to read the book as a whole. Sometimes, in a blow, the waves rose like great hills, and the captain would hold the wheel with white knuckles, our bow one minute plunging gigantically down into a valley of green water, the next moment reaching the bottom of the trough and soaring upwards towards the sky before topping the next crest and starting down again.

Early in my career as a deck hand, I had read the Hazel Barnes translation of Jean Paul Sartre's *Being and Nothingness,* in which he argued that phenomena only arose for consciousness in the existential context of human projects, a theme that recalled Marx's 1844 manuscripts, where nature was "produced" by man, meaning, for example, that when the mystic sees a stand of trees, his consciousness hypostatizes an entirely different phenomenal object than a poet does, for example, or a capitalist. To the mystic, it is a manifestation; to the poet, a forest; to the capitalist, lumber. According to such a perspective, a mountain only appears as tall in the context of the project of climbing it, and so on, according to the instrumental relations involved in various human interests. But the great natural events of the sea surrounding us seemed to defy, with their stubborn, irreducible facticity, our uncomprehending attempts to come to terms with them. Suddenly, we were just there, shaken by the forces around us without making sense of them, wondering if we would make it through. Some, it was true, would ask God's help at such moments, but when we returned safely to shore, we behaved like men who knew little of Him, as if those moments had been a lapse into insanity, embarrassing to think of at happier times. It was one of the lessons of the sea that in fact, such events not only existed but perhaps even preponderated in our life. Man was small and weak, the forces around him were large, and he did not control them.

Sometimes a boat would sink and men would die. I remember a fisherman from another boat who was working near us one opening, doing the same job as I did, piling web. He smiled across the water as he pulled the net from the hydraulic block overhead, stacking it neatly on the stern to ready it for the next set. Some weeks later, his boat overturned while fishing in a storm, and he got caught in the web and drowned. I saw him only once again, in a dream, beckoning to me from the stern of his boat.

The tremendousness of the scenes we lived in, the storms, the towering sheer cliffs rising vertically out of the water for hundreds of feet, the cold and rain and fatigue, the occasional injuries and deaths of workers—these made little impression on most of us. Fishermen were, after all, supposed to be tough. On one boat, the family that worked it was said to lose an occasional crew member while running at sea at the end of the season, invariably the sole nonfamily member who worked with them, his "loss" saving them the wages they would have otherwise had to pay him.

The captain of another was a twenty-seven-year-old who delivered millions of dollars worth of crab each year in the Bering Sea. When I first heard of him, we were in Kodiak, his boat at the city dock they had tied up to after a lengthy run some days before. The captain was presently indisposed in his bunk in the stateroom, where he had been vomiting up blood from having eaten a glass uptown the previous night to prove how tough he was.

He was in somewhat better condition when I later saw him in the Bering Sea at the end of a long winter king crab season. He worked in his wheelhouse up top, surrounded by radios that could pull in a signal from just about anywhere, computers, Loran, sonar, depth-finders, radar. His panels of lights and switches were set below the 180-degree sweep of shatterproof windows that over-looked the sea and the men on deck below, to whom he communicated by loudspeaker. They often worked round the clock, pulling their gear up from the icy water under watchful batteries of enormous electric lights attached to the masts that turned the perpetual night of the winter months into day. The captain had a reputation as a screamer, and had once locked his crew out on deck in the rain for eleven hours because one of them had gone inside to have a cup of coffee without permission. Few crewmen lasted longer than a season with him, though they made nearly twice the yearly income of, say, a lawyer or an advertising executive, and in only six months. Fortunes were made in the Bering Sea in those years, before over-fishing wiped out the crab.

At present, he was at anchor, and was amiable enough when we tied up to him and he came aboard to sit and talk with our own captain. They spoke at length, at times gazing thoughtfully out at the sea through the door or windows, at times looking at each other sharply when something animated them, as the topic of what his competitors thought of him now did. "They wonder why I have a few bucks," he said. "Well, I slept in my own home one night last year."

He later had his crew throw off the lines and pick the anchor, his eyes flickering warily over the water from the windows of the house as he pulled away with a blast of smoke from the stack. His watchfulness, his walrus-like physique, his endless voyages after game and markets, reminded me of other predatory hunter-animals of the sea. Such people, good at making money but heedless of any ultimate end or purpose, made an impression on me, and

I increasingly began to wonder if men didn't need principles to guide them and tell them why they were there. Without such principles, nothing seemed to distinguish us above our prey except being more thorough, and technologically capable of preying longer, on a vaster scale, and with greater devastation than the animals we hunted.

These considerations were in my mind the second year I studied at Chicago, where I became aware through studies of philosophical moral systems that philosophy had not been successful in the past at significantly influencing people's morals and preventing injustice, and I came to realize that there was little hope for it to do so in the future. I found that comparing human cultural systems and societies in their historical succession and multiplicity had led many intellectuals to moral relativism, since no moral value could be discovered which on its own merits was transculturally valid, a reflection leading to nihilism, the perspective that sees human civilizations as plants that grow out of the earth, springing from their various seeds and soils, thriving for a time, and then dying away.

Some heralded this as intellectual liberation, among them Emile Durkheim in his *Elementary Forms of the Religious Life,* or Sigmund Freud in his *Totem and Taboo,* which discussed mankind as if it were a patient and diagnosed its religious traditions as a form of a collective neurosis that we could now hope to cure, by applying to them a thorough-going scientific atheism, a sort of salvation through "pure science."

On this subject, I bought the Jeremy Shapiro translation of *Knowledge and Human Interests* by Jürgen Habermas, who argued that there was no such thing as "pure science" that could be depended upon to forge boldly ahead in a steady improvement of itself and the world. He called such a misunderstanding *scientism*, not science. Science in the real world, he said, was not free of values, still less of interests. The kinds of research that obtain funding, for example, were a function of what their society deemed meaningful, expedient, profitable, or important. Habermas had been of a generation of German academics who, during the thirties and forties, knew what was happening in their country, but insisted they were simply engaged in "intellectual production," that they were living in the realm of "scholarship," and need not concern themselves with whatever the state might choose to do with their research. The horrible question mark that was attached to German intellectuals when the Nazi atrocities became public after the war made Habermas think deeply about the ideology of "pure science." If anything was obvious, it was that the nineteenth-century optimism of thinkers like Freud and Durkheim was no longer tenable.

I began to reassess the intellectual life around me. Like Schopenhauer, I felt that higher education must produce higher human beings. But at the university, I found lab people talking to each other about forging research data to secure funding for the coming year; luminaries who wouldn't permit tape recorders at their lectures for fear that competitors in the same field would "go one step further" with their research and beat them to publication; professors vying with each other in the length of their courses' syllabuses. The moral qualities I was accustomed to associate with ordinary, unregenerate humanity seemed as frequently met with in sophisticated academics as they had been in fishermen. If one could laugh at fishermen who, after getting a boatload of fish in a big catch, would cruise back and forth in front of the others to let them see how laden down in the water they were, ostensibly "looking for more fish"; what could one say about the P.h.D's who behaved the same way about their books and articles? I felt that their knowledge had not developed their persons, that the secret of higher man did not lie in their sophistication.

I wondered if I hadn't gone down the road of philosophy as far as one could go. While it had debunked my Christianity and provided some genuine insights, it had not yet answered the big questions. Moreover, I felt that this was somehow connected—I didn't know whether as cause or effect—to the fact that our intellectual tradition no longer seemed to seriously comprehend itself. What were any of us, whether philosophers, fishermen, garbagemen, or kings, except bit players in a drama we did not understand, diligently playing out our roles until our replacements were sent, and we gave our last performance? But could one legitimately hope for more than this? I read Kojève's *Introduction to the Reading of Hegel,* in which he explained that for Hegel, philosophy did not culminate in the system, but rather in the Wise Man, someone able to answer any possible question on the ethical implications of human actions. This made me consider our own plight in the twentieth century, which could no longer answer a single ethical question.

It was thus as if this century's unparalleled mastery of concrete things had somehow ended by making us things. I contrasted this with Hegel's concept of the "concrete" in his *Phenomenology of Mind*. An example of the abstract, in his terms, was the limitary physical reality of the book now held in your hands, while the concrete was its interconnection with the larger realities it presupposed, the modes of production that determined the kind of ink and paper in it, the aesthetic standards that dictated its design, the systems of marketing and distribution that had carried it to the reader, the historical circumstances that had brought about the reader's literacy and taste; the cultural events that had mediated its style and usage; in short, the "bigger picture" in which it was articulated and had its being. For Hegel, the movement of philosophical investigation always led from the abstract to the concrete, to the more real. He was therefore able to say that philosophy necessarily led to theology, whose object was the ultimately real, the Deity. This seemed to me to point up an irreducible lack in our century. I began to wonder if, by materializing our culture and our past, we had not somehow abstracted ourselves from our wider humanity, from our true nature in relation to a higher reality.

At this juncture, I read a number of works on Islam, among them the books of Seyyed Hossein Nasr, who believed that many of the problems of western man, especially those of the environment, were from his having left the divine wisdom of revealed religion, which taught him his true place as a creature of God in the natural world and to understand and respect it. Without it, he burned

up and consumed nature with ever more effective tech-
nological styles of commercial exploitation that ruined
his world from without while leaving him increasingly
empty within, because he did not know why he existed or
to what end he should act.

I reflected that this might be true as far as it went, but it
begged the question as to the truth of revealed religion.
Everything on the face of the earth, all moral and religious
systems, were on the same plane, unless one could gain
certainty that one of them was from a higher source,
the sole guarantee of the objectivity, the whole force, of
moral law. Otherwise, one man's opinion was as good as
another's, and we remained in an undifferentiated sea of
conflicting individual interests, in which no valid objec-
tion could be raised to the strong eating the weak.

I read other books on Islam, and came across some
passages translated by W. Montgomery Watt from *That
Which Delivers from Error* by the theologian and mystic
al-Ghazali, who, after a midlife crisis of questioning and
doubt, realized that "beyond the light of prophetic revelation there is no other light on the face of the earth from
which illumination may be received," the very point to
which my philosophical inquiries had led. Here was, in
Hegel's terms, the Wise Man, in the person of a divinely
inspired messenger who alone had the authority to answer
questions of good and evil.

I also read A. J. Arberry's translation *The Koran
Interpreted,* and I recalled my early wish for a sacred book.
Even in translation, the superiority of the Muslim scripture
over the Bible was evident in every line, as if the reality of

divine revelation, dimly heard of all my life, had now been placed before my eyes. In its exalted style, its power, its inexorable finality, its uncanny way of anticipating the arguments of the atheistic heart in advance and answering them; it was a clear exposition of God as God and man as man, the revelation of the awe-inspiring Divine Unity being the identical revelation of social and economic justice among men.

I began to learn Arabic at Chicago, and after studying the grammar for a year with a fair degree of success, decided to take a leave of absence to try to advance in the language in a year of private study in Cairo. Too, a desire for new horizons drew me, and after a third season of fishing, I went to the Middle East.

In Egypt, I found something I believe brings many to Islam, namely, the mark of pure monotheism upon its followers, which struck me as more profound than anything I had previously encountered. I met many Muslims in Egypt, good and bad, but all influenced by the teachings of their Book to a greater extent than I had ever seen elsewhere. It has been some twenty-four years since then, and I cannot remember them all, or even most of them, but perhaps the ones I can recall will serve to illustrate the impressions made.

One was a man on the side of the Nile near the Miqyas Gardens, where I used to walk. I came upon him praying on a piece of cardboard, facing across the water. I started to pass in front of him, but suddenly checked myself and walked around behind, not wanting to disturb him. As I watched a moment before going my way, I beheld a man absorbed in his relation to God, oblivious to my presence, much less my opinions about him or his religion. To my mind, there was something magnificently detached about this, altogether strange for someone coming from the West, where praying in public was virtually the only thing that remained obscene.

Another was a young boy from secondary school who greeted me near Khan al-Khalili, and because I spoke some Arabic and he spoke some English and wanted to tell me about Islam, he walked with me several miles across town to Giza, explaining as much as he could. When we parted, I think he said a prayer that I might become Muslim.

Another was a Yemeni friend living in Cairo who brought me a copy of the Koran at my request to help me learn Arabic. I did not have a table beside the chair where I used to sit and read in my hotel room, and it was my custom to stack the books on the floor. When I set the Koran by the others there, he silently stooped and picked it up, out of respect for it. This impressed me because I knew he was not religious, but here was the effect of Islam upon him.

Another was a woman I met while walking beside a bicycle on an unpaved road on the opposite side of the Nile from Luxor. I was dusty, and somewhat shabbily clothed, and she was an old woman dressed in black from head to toe who walked up, and without a word or glance at me, pressed a coin into my hand so suddenly that in my surprise I dropped it. By the time I picked it up, she had hurried away. Because she thought I was poor, even if obviously non-Muslim, she gave me some money without any expectation for it except what was between her and her God. This act made me think a lot about Islam, because nothing seemed to have motivated her but that.

Many other things passed through my mind during the months I stayed in Egypt to learn Arabic. I found myself thinking that a man must have some sort of religion, and I was more impressed by the effect of Islam on the lives of Muslims, a certain nobility of purpose and largesse of soul, than I had ever been by any other religion's or even atheism's effect on its followers. The Muslims seemed to have more than we did.

Christianity had its good points to be sure, but they seemed mixed with confusions, and I found myself more and more inclined to look to Islam for their fullest and most perfect expression. The first question we had memorized from our early catechism had been "Why were you created?" to which the correct answer was "To know, love, and serve God." When I reflected on those around me, I realized that Islam, not Christianity, furnished the most comprehensive and understandable way to practice this on a daily basis.

As for the inglorious political fortunes of the Muslims today, I did not feel these to be a reproach against Islam, or to relegate it to an inferior position in a "natural order" of world ideologies, but rather saw them as a low phase in a larger cycle of history. Foreign hegemony over Muslim lands had been witnessed before in the thoroughgoing destruction of Islamic civilization in the thirteenth century by the Mongol horde, who razed cities and built pyramids of human heads from the steppes of Central Asia to the Muslim heartlands, after which the fullness of destiny brought forth the Ottoman Empire to raise the Word of Allah and make it a vibrant political reality that endured for centuries. It was now, I reflected, merely the turn of contemporary Muslims to strive for a new historic crystallization of Islam, something one might well aspire to share in.

When a friend in Cairo one day asked me, "Why don't you become a Muslim," I found that Allah had created within me a desire to belong to this religion, which so enriches its followers, from the simplest hearts to the most magisterial intellects. It is not through an act of the mind or will that anyone becomes a Muslim, but rather through the mercy of Allah, and this, in the final analysis, was what brought me to Islam in Cairo in 1977.

> Is it not time that the hearts of those
> who believe should be humbled to the
> Remembrance of God and the Truth which
> He has sent down, and that they should
> not be as those to whom the Book was
> given aforetime, and the term seemed
> over long to them, so that their hearts
> have become hard, and many of them
> are ungodly?
> Know that God revives the earth after
> it was dead. We have indeed made clear
> for you the signs, that haply you will
> understand.
> (Koran 57:16–17)

THE MUSLIM BELIEF IN GOD

AL-GHAZALI

HIS ONENESS

He is one in being without partner, unique without peer, ultimate without opposite, alone without equal. He is one, preeternal, beginninglessly uncreate, everlastingly abiding, unceasingly existent, eternally limitless, the ever self-subsisting through whom all else subsists, ever enduring, without end. He is, was, and ever will be possessed of all attributes of majesty, unannihilated by dissolution or separation through the passage of eons or terminus of interims. He is the First and Last, the Outward and Inward, and He has knowledge of everything.

HIS TRANSCENDENCE

He is not a body with a form, or a limitary, quantitative substance, not resembling bodies in quantifiability or divisibility, or in being a substance or qualified by substance, or being an accident or qualified by accidents. He does not resemble anything that exists, nor anything that exists resemble Him. There is nothing whatsoever like unto Him, nor is He like unto anything. He is not delimited by magnitude, contained by places, encompassed by directions, or bounded by heavens or earth. He is 'ascendant over the Throne' (*mustawin*, Koran 20:5) in the way He says and the meaning He intends, 'ascendant' in a manner transcending contact, settledness, position, indwelling, or movement. The Throne does not bear Him up, but is borne up by the subtlety of His infinite power, as are the angels who carry it, and all are powerless in His grasp. He is above the Throne, the heavens, and all else to the farthest reaches of the stars, with an aboveness that does not increase His nearness to the Throne or the heavens, or His distance from the earth and what lies beneath it. He is as exalted in degree above the Throne and the heavens as He is above the earth and its depths, though He is near to everything in existence, nearer to a servant than his own jugular vein, and is witness to everything. His nearness no more resembles the nearness of objects to one another than His entity resembles the entities of objects. He does not indwell in anything, nor anything indwell in Him. He is as exalted above containment in space as He is above confinement in time. He was, before creating time and space, and is now even as He was. He is distinguished from His creation by His attributes. There is nothing in His entity other than Him, nor is His entity in what is other than Him. He is beyond change and motion: events neither occur within Him nor changes befall Him. He remains in His attributes of majesty exalted above change, and in the attributes of His perfection beyond needing any increase in perfection. The existence of His entity is known by human reason, and in the afterlife is beheld by the eyesight of the righteous as a beatitude and favor, to consummate their perfect joy with the sight of His Noble Countenance.

HIS LIFE AND ALMIGHTY POWER

He Most High is living, almighty, overmastering, triumphant, unaffected by inability or weakness; unsusceptible to drowsiness, sleep, annihilation, or death; possessed of absolute sovereignty and might, of irresistible power and force. His is the majesty and sway, the creation and command. The heavens are enfolded in His right hand and all beings are powerless in His grasp. He alone creates, begins, gives existence, and originates. He creates all beings and their acts, ordains their sustenance and terms. Nothing possible is out of His grasp, the disposal of no matter is beyond His power. The number of things He can do is limitless, the amount He knows is infinite.

HIS KNOWLEDGE

He knows all things knowable, encompassing all that takes place from the depths of the earth to the highest heaven. He knows without an atom's weight in the earth or heavens escaping His knowledge. He knows the creeping of black ant across a great stone on a lightless night, and the motion in the air of a particle of dust on a windy day. He knows the concealed and the yet more hidden, the buried recesses of hearts, the movement of thought, and the opacities of the inmost soul; with preeternal, beginningless knowledge that He has always possessed from the limitless reaches of past eternity, not with awareness originating within Him through being imparted or conveyed.

He Most High wills all that exists and directs all events. Nothing occurs in the physical or spiritual world, be it meager or much, little or great, good or evil, of benefit or detriment, faith or unbelief, knowledge or ignorance, triumph or ruin, increase or decrease, obedience or sin; save through His ordinance, apportionment, wisdom, and decision. What He wills is, and what He does not will is not. Neither sidelong glance nor passing thought is beyond His design. He originates all and returns it, does what He wills, and none can repulse His command. There is no rescinding His destiny, no flight for a servant from disobeying Him except through divinely given success therein and mercy, and no strength to obey Him save through His choice and decree. If all mankind, jinn, angels, and devils combined their efforts to move or to still a single particle of the universe without His will and choice, they would be unable to. His will, like His other attributes, exists in His entity and He ever possesses it. He has willed from preeternity the existence of all things at the times He has chosen. They occur at the times which He has destined from beginingless eternity, occurring neither before nor after, but taking place in accordance with His knowledge and will, without substitution or alteration. He directs events without successive thoughts or waiting for time to elapse, which is why nothing diverts Him from anything else.

He Most High is all-hearing and all-seeing. He hears and sees, no sound however slight eluding His hearing, and no sight however minute escaping His vision. Distance does not obscure His hearing nor darkness hinder His vision. He sees without pupil or eyelids, and hears without ear canal or ears, just as He knows without a heart, seizes without limb, and creates without implement. His attributes no more resemble the attributes of His creatures than His entity resembles the entity of His creatures.

HIS SPEECH

He Most High speaks, commands, forbids, promises, and warns with beginninglessly eternal speech that is an attribute of His entity, not resembling the speech of creatures in being a sound generated by the passage of air or impact of bodies nor in letters articulated by compressing the lips or moving the tongue. The Koran, Torah, Evangel, and Psalms are His Books, revealed to His messengers (upon whom be peace). The Koran is recited with tongues, written in books, and memorized in hearts despite being beginninglessly eternal, an attribute of the entity of Allah Most High, unsubject to disseverance and separation by conveyance to hearts or pages. Moses (Allah bless him and give him peace) heard the speech of Allah without sound or letter, just as the righteous see the entity of Allah Most High in the afterlife without substance or accident.

Since Allah possesses all of the above attributes, He is

living, knowing, omnipotent, willing, hearing, seeing, and speaking by virtue of His life, power, knowledge, will, hearing, sight, and speech, not merely by virtue of His entity.

Everything besides Him Glorious and Exalted exists through His action, proceeding from His justice in the best, fullest, most perfect and equitable way. He is wise in His acts and just in His decrees. His justice is not comparable to the justice of His servants, since injustice may only be imagined from a servant through his disposal of what belongs to another, while this is inconceivable from Allah Most High, since nothing belongs to anyone besides Him that He should unjustly dispose of it.

Everything besides Him, be it human, jinn, angel, devil, heaven, earth, animal, vegetable, mineral, substance, accident, intelligible, or sensory, is contingent, and was brought into existence through His power after not being, created by Him after it was nothing. He alone existed in preeternity, and nothing else. He then originated creation, that His omnipotence might be manifest, His prior decree effected, and His eternal word realized; not from needing or requiring anything in creation. Our origination, beginning, and responsibility are of Allah's generosity, not because of their being obligatory for Him, and His blessings and benefaction exist because of His favor, not because of being due from Him. Everything that exists is indebted to Him for His generosity and goodness, His blessings and benevolence; for He is well able to pour all manner of torments upon His servants and try them with every variety of suffering and illness, and were He to do so, it would be just on His part and not wicked or unfair. He Mighty and Majestic rewards His servants, the believers, for their acts of obedience because of His generosity and in fulfillment of His word, not because of their deserving it or His owing it to them. He is not obliged to anyone to do anything, nor is injustice on His part conceivable, for He does not owe any rights to anyone. The obligation of men and jinn to perform acts of obedience is established by His having informed them of it upon the tongues of the prophets (upon whom be peace), and not by unaided human reason. He sent the prophets and manifested the truth of their messages by unmistakable, inimitable miracles. They have communicated His commands, prohibitions, promises, and warnings, and it is obligatory for mankind and jinn to believe in what they have conveyed.

HIS MESSENGER

Allah Most High sent Muhammad (Allah bless him and give him peace), the Qurayshite unlettered prophet, to deliver His inspired message to the entire world, Arabs and non-Arabs, jinn and mankind, superseding and abrogating all previous religious systems with the Prophet's sacred law, except for the provisions of them that the new revelation explicitly reconfirmed. Allah favored him above the other prophets and made him the highest of mankind, rejecting anyone's attesting to the divine oneness by saying "There is no god but Allah," unless they also attest to the Prophet by saying "Muhammad is the Messenger of Allah." He has obliged men and jinn to believe everything the Prophet (Allah bless him and give him peace) has informed us concerning this world and the next, and does not accept anyone's faith unless they believe in what he has told us will happen after death . . . .

✳

(Translated by the author from the Arabic of the *Ihya' 'ulum al-din* [Giving life to the religious sciences] of Abu Hamid al-Ghazali [d. 1111AD], 1:79–81. 4 vols. Cairo, 1929.)